The Nature of of Night

By Jennifer Gordon

Curious Corvid Publishing, Ohio

Curious Corvid
PUBLISHING

The Nature of Night by Jennifer Gordon

Published by Curious Corvid Publishing, LLC.

Copyright © 2022 by Jennifer Gordon

Cover design by Mark Alexander McClish @markmakesart247

Photo by MAD Five O Photography
Interior photos licensed through Shutterstock
Author photo by Kailey Hein Photography

Printed in the United States of America
Cataloging-in-Publication Data is on file with the Library of Congress.
ISBN: 979-8-9863003-5-1
www.curiouscorvidpublishing.com

You can find more of Jennifer's poetry on Instagram
@jennifergordonpoetry

Prologue

There is no such thing as permanence. No thought, nor feeling, nor state of mind has the nature to withstand the endless passage of time. Not a human on earth is a creature of linear emotion. Like the river, we are fluid and winding. Like the trees, ever changing. Even a connection that lasts a lifetime will go through phases that wax and wane. Moments of darkness and moments of bliss. And what a comfort it can be, to know there is more in the distance. To know the sun will rise again, no matter how black the night has been. What a relief it has been to my soul, to learn the art of acceptance. To hold a moment in my hand and treasure its presence as a fleeting thing. Depression, anxiety, rage, hate, love, lust, even pain. Each seemingly all consuming. Each giving the illusion of always existing. But the facade is not to be believed. What is bold and bright will eventually fade. What begins as a seed will one day leave the soil behind. So my advice, is to love the beautiful moments for what they are offering you in the present. Whether or not they last forever, cherish them for what they are today. Recognize the moments of pain and sadness as beings of temporary existence. Meditate on wisdom. Remember who you are. Remember how far you have come. Search the stars for lessons meant to be yours and be kind to yourself amidst the darkness.

Chapter 1:
Goodnight Sunlight

Sadness
slips into my veins
and the light of my heart
is laid to sleep

Jennifer Gordon

I had always understood the concept of grief
as one might understand the wilderness
by observing the life of a single tree
But is there truly any comprehension
in such a distant means of observation?

Not until it crashes down upon your home
can you truly absorb what it means to grieve
Not until you are lost in the vastness of the wild
can you understand the magnitude
of a hundred thousand trees

Goodnight sunlight
my old friend
I shall await your presence
through the night

Until we meet again

This world holds too much concrete
Never enough maturing trees
And far too many dying dreams

I feel as though
I was set on fire
years ago
Gasoline skin
and paper wings
Reduced to ashes
of foolish dreams

If love is an ocean
then I am nothing
but debris
A lonesome piece
of wreckage
drifting amidst
the lies I believed

They say we either
sink or swim
but I have been drowning
for years
Beaten and bruised
by the tides of time
Sustaining life
through shallow breaths
So it seems as though
they didn't know
that some of us can stay afloat
by holding on
to scraps of hope

I see you, my friend
struggling with sorrow

So I have decided
to put away my
rose-colored glasses
and find a pair
of tinted blue

So I may view
the world with you

I want to hear more than just your words
I want to feel the things you cannot say

Pry open your doubts
Cradle your pain

I want to expose the depths of your soul
Know every demon you hide away

And then, my love
I want to stay

I wish I knew how to touch you
but you are cocooned in solitude
inside a tomb of hand laid stone
A darkness born of self-made relics

How am I to embrace your heart
when my arms can only reach so far?
How am I to help you breathe
when you have turned your back on me?

Well, my love
I am not so easily prone to abandon
Unwilling to allow
the waste of your burial

I will sit in silence
Mediate for guidance
And await the day you understand
you have captured a heart
who will always love you

No matter how many ways we try
the tears we cry won't turn back time

We don't always get a final goodbye

They see the world
through a lens of clarity
I see it all
through a lens of grief
So I find it hard
to describe the view
when none of them
have ever known
what it means to lose
someone like you

I absorb too much
Hold on too long
Store too many memories
in my bones

My breaths are shallow
when the rivers are deep
And I cannot seem to shake
your voice from my dreams

I write your name on the riverbank
dragging fingertips through the sand

A desperate attempt
to prove you still belong in my hands

But I know the waters will wash it away
Sinking slowly, gently corroding

And deep down
I know your role in my life was the same

The truth is
I always knew you couldn't stay

Jennifer Gordon

I swear
I can hear you in the rain

The sound of your voice
cutting through the atmosphere

Echos of your indifferent reply
as the cloud formation continues to cry

I cannot help but wonder
if she knows what it is like to love you

Tell me
Did you break her heart too?

I am embers in the clouds
Remnants of a fire long since extinguished
Floating freely towards the heavens
Caught in the ebb of gentle winds

I am burnt into weightlessness
Becoming smaller bits of nothing
Losing warmth while gaining distance
Gone from the thoughts of ghosts

I am neither here nor there
Specks of dust in the open air
Ashes tapped from his cigar
A brittle heart becoming stars

Intimacy means opening
and so for some
becomes more burden
than elation
More hesitation
than reception
For every broken heart
has learned
The world feels like a safer place
when our doors
are locked at night

They say there is hope in knowing
that distance has its limits
That we are both beneath the same
blanket of stars each night
But I know better
I know this void is far too wide
for building bridges in the sky

Tonight I realized
that I could not remember
the last time I had eaten

It may have been hours
Maybe more
Maybe since yesterday

And the huger in my belly
had spread into my bones

And it felt a lot
like missing you

No matter how many times
I bury your name beneath the soil
Always
Your memory claims itself as a seed
and again you bloom inside my dreams

I was not built for days like these
My flesh is a home to fragile things
I am matchstick ribs and a heart of string

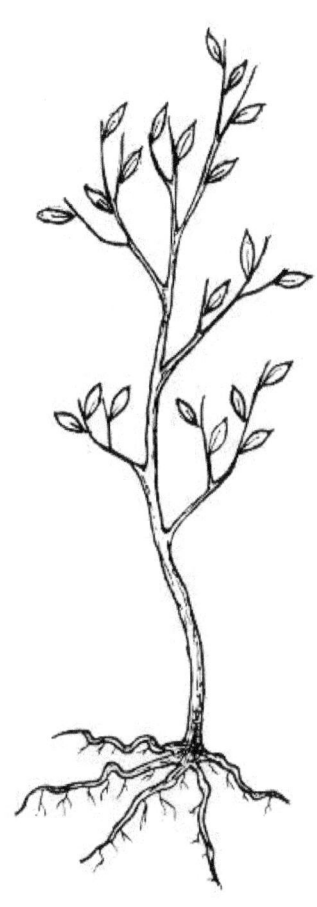

Jennifer Gordon

Observing a sky of endless stars
and my heavy heart cannot help but feel
that you are even farther
from my arms than they are

You are the sunset
in my rear-view mirror
While I am nothing
but a smudge
on the reflection of memories
you would rather see

I would write a hundred thousand poems
if I thought my words would bring you home

Absence has a way
of making its presence known
by carving names
of the dead and gone
into the structure of living bones

Jennifer Gordon

Even the most wild of flowers
will wither away without the rain

I am not afraid of letting go
but I fear the absence of myself
And if I release
the pieces of me
that still belong to you
I know there will be nothing left

No more of me
to hold onto

Weak and weary
under heaven
I gather what remains
and as the smoke
begins to clear
I open my arms
to the coming rain

Chapter Two:
Tracing Constellations

I am left
with nothing but time
to connect the complexities
of the human mind

I wish I was better
at burning bridges
At setting fire
to the strings of my heart
that cling to things
which served me long ago

I wish I was better
at letting go
Detaching from the bonds
that used to hold me
but are no longer soft
upon my skin

I wish I was better
at knowing my own soul
Unfolding the edges
of notes my thoughts
have tucked within my ribs

Reading the words out loud
that have taken shelter
beneath my tongue

Some things simply refuse
to be let go
They become a part of you
A hurt
brutally etched
into your bones
But we keep moving forward
one shaking step
in front of the other
because the burdens of brokenness
are simply not enough
to stop the passage of time

They say that love is a choice
and I find myself in disagreement
Loyalty is a choice
Devotion is a choice
Effort is a choice
And while these are decisions
that often stem from a place of love
they are not love themselves
Love is not a choice of the mind
it is a condition of the heart
And the heart cares nothing
for logic nor institution
for reason nor absolution
It is a feral state of being
recklessly independent
from the mere human efforts
of guided direction

Jennifer Gordon

I am but an ember of cosmic fires
A flicker of warmth
In the seasons of eternity

I turn and run
when I glimpse the sun
Fearing its warmth
may strike a match
and I know how quickly
dead things burn

I haven't left this life quite yet
but I know my bones
hold the scent of death
For they are parched
and drained of substance
Hung out to dry
in a barren wilderness
Labeled too far gone
for saving

So who am I
to reach for the sky
when the only story
my heart has known
is the tale of a woman
who walks alone

Studying stars
is an infinite art
Nearly as vast
as the human heart

When I said that I would
always love you
I meant that you have
made it impossible not to

That you have
captured me in ways
that have left my soul
irreversibly changed

That every time I see my
own reflection in the mirror
I look into the eyes of someone
who has never seen anyone
more beautiful than you

Sometimes
the angel
and the enemy
are not as different
as they seem

And like the dandelion
I have scattered

Reduced to seedlings drained of color
From woman in bloom to a tumble of words
and every piece now clings to the breeze
Whisked away through moments of time
Landing upon the open plains
On crooked paths and riverbanks

The winds of life
may believe they have won
but I am not one to remain undone

The nature of a wildflower is not to wither
but to spread its beauty upon the world
and come back stronger
every time
Even more wild
than she was before

As difficult as it is to suffer
I believe sometimes the deepest pain
graciously serves as a treasured reminder
of how immensely beautiful
whatever we lost had been

So in a way

Perhaps this perpetual aching in my ribs
is actually a gift
A memento from the echoes of the universe
of a time when I was granted witness
to something real and profound

Something that the rest of the world
can only open a book of poems
and read about

The instinctual pull
of my own wild heart
is the only compass
I long to follow

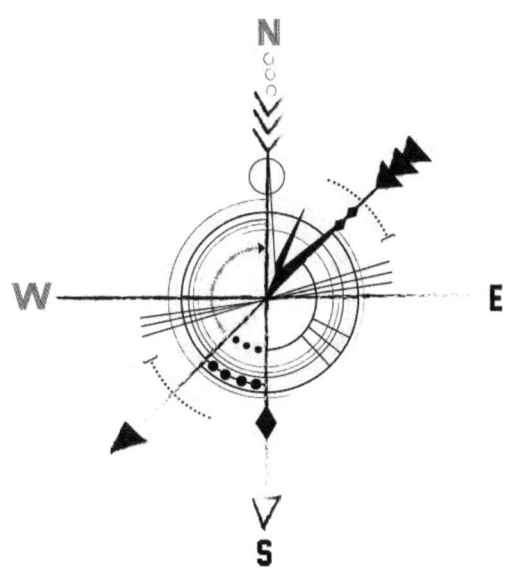

Lovers always speak
to the beauty of the moon

And yet her light is not her own
She merely reflects a generous sun

But even a burning, golden hue
is pale in comparison

To the way my eyes see you

Show me
the infinite intricacies
of mathematics
the limitless specifics
of quantum physics
and still
I will hold my ground
in knowing
there is simply nothing
more profound
than the vastness of
the human heart

I believe in extraordinary things
Like heaven and hell
The saints who fell
And demons with white wings

Maybe the madness
is built upon more than sadness
Maybe the undercurrent of less than normal
has always been a present fog
floating from the inside out
And maybe the reasons I fear the dark
have less to do with the presence of evil
and more to do with my own heart

What if these poems are hollow logs
Carved upon by foolish love
Caving in, from hidden cracks
Crumbling from the outside in

What happens when you learn
That I am nothing but an echo
A hesitant vibration
Lost between translations

Where will meaning sink its roots
If planted words bear withered fruit
And how am I to leave my mark
If we are but a passing mist
Tracing shadows in the dark

Please don't tell me
which way to go

My soul already knows

I will follow wherever
the wild wind blows

I am neither lost nor found
though I have never known the name
of this road I am on
It stretches forth through present time
and I often pause
to observe what is mine
Footprints along the surface past
are born of dirt and bits of earth
Proof that my feet
have often wandered from the pavement
And the road ahead will be no different
Some days the world will find me
walking boldly towards the horizon
Other times
I will be but a shadow
off and running
with the forest wolves

Every time I think I belong
this road I'm on
stretches farther along

I shy away
from things with edges
Sharpened tongues
Emotional ledges
Retreating
within the confines
Of my own
makeshift trenches
Burrowing deep
into layers of debris
Layers of whatever
is left of me
Desperately longing
for safety
For the strength to
bury this anxiety
Tuck it warmly
within my heart
and hide my fears
under piled stones
Let them rest
in the softness
of darkness
As this broken shell
I call my bones
finds the courage
to emerge from home

Even when invited
I second guess
the nature of being wanted
Overthink their efforts
of inclusion
As if perhaps
my presence is a burden
And who am I
to believe I might belong

My dreams in life are simple
I long only to be an island
A self-sustaining piece of earth
Surrounded by a raging sea
Drowning the pirates who come for me

But even an island
Is merely an illusion of isolation
Touched upon by wind and sun
A living, breathing frailty
Always at the mercy of the elements

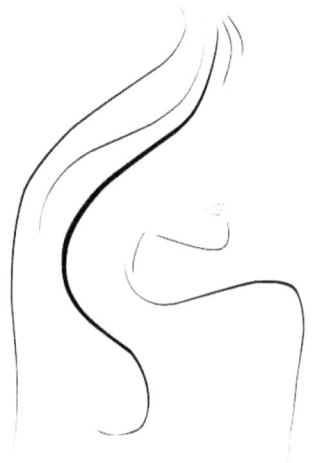

I spend far too much time
creating scenarios in my mind
Fearing the fallouts that never come
Chasing closure
as if my thoughts could serve as arrows
in the hunt
Reading too much
into other people's movements
only to find I have interpreted
things all wrong
Again
Being surprised
by lies I had not foreseen
Despite my constant attempts
to spot the bombs before they drop
I spend too much time
looking out instead of in
Yearning for acceptance
from those who hold no stake
in the fruits of my existence
I know these things
and yet I drift
Constantly engaging in the balance
between the sweetness of wisdom
and the salt of wounds
where hell has bloomed

Maybe the path towards peace of mind
is less about which way you go
and more about the courage to walk there alone

I am an over producer of things
designed to thrive in smaller doses
Affection towards strangers
who give the slightest hint of connection
Ounces of wine in glasses stained
by the constant imprint of my fingertips
Hours lost in page after page
of another author's creative space
Waves of grief
for moments seemingly long since forgotten
by everyone but myself
Hunting for morsels of passion
to fill a stomach starving for substance
Daydreams leading me far from home
even when I know they hold no tangibility
I over share, over feel, over crave
day after day
giving more of myself than I dare to take

I am sorry
I have nothing left
to offer you
what once was mine
was stolen
by a man who spoke
in beautiful lies
So I may appear
to the naked eye
as a woman
with a heart to give
But truly
I am nothing but a shell
A lovely ghost
Who hides it well

I have made my peace
with darkness

It is light who hesitates

To accept the burden
of my presence

I watch the wild ways
of backyard birds
from the comfort of
my windowpane
And I cannot help
but wonder
if the angels watch me
in a similar way
Observing every
failed attempt
at collecting crumbs
to feed the soul
Smiling at
the rare event
where I let my wings
control the fall

I have believed in the
goodness of others
to a fault
My hopeful heart
has fallen for so
many lines
Swallowed the poison
of so many lies
So I am not quite sure
how to feel anymore
when someone dares
place a promise
upon my ears
I long to wrap
my heart in their words
But self-preservation
is a thinning line
and though I am young
I feel I have lost
more faith
than anyone should
in a single lifetime

Sometimes the moon and the sun
hover together in a sky made for one
And I wonder why
What has made them decide
to share their space today
Perhaps if I were smarter, wiser
I would understand
the science behind such things
But I am a simple woman
Built not for solving riddles
but for spending my days
gazing in awe
at the million mysteries of the world

Amidst the crowds, I am a lonely soul
Only in solitude, do I feel at home

Amongst the beasts and towering trees
Babbling brooks and singing streams

I seek companions, perched in branches
Grin at the birds I call my kin

As I swim in rivers of calming waters
And bathe in the fragrance of floral colors

The wild has claimed me as her own
Branded by the notches of peace in my bones

The Nature of Night

So often we fail
to see the forest for the trees
Not because we lack a view
of the world in birth
of beautiful things
But because we are taught
to tilt our eyes
down from the morning sun
as she shines
and who can build
a perspective of growth
when the ground is all
we ever know?

To fall is to begin
Begin a process of becoming
Becoming what, or whom
Now there is the element of risk

Observe the rain in all its glory
Swan driving, carelessly falling
From the safety of the clouds
Out into the great unknown

Cascading towards destiny
Merging as one with the ocean tides
Landing on lashes of forest beasts
Forming rivers in city streets

How I crave the rush of fate
The plunging, tumbling of my soul
Free falling
Towards the woman I shall become

I have been the tree
Sturdy in my roots
Standing tall
A living statue in the storm

I have been the leaves
Scattered by winds
Lost
Muted color beneath the frost

Perhaps one day
I will be the seeds
Secrets buried within the earth
A promise yet to bloom

May madness become you at least once in life
So you may discover the rifts in your soul
The dangers lurking below your control
And may you emerge both courageous and humble
Walking with the grace of one who has stumbled

Chapter 3:
Shifting Shadows

The warmth of morning
nudges my soul
and I wake to find
the sun at my door

Jennifer Gordon

Daybreak slips above the trees
Lending light in tranquil spills
And as I watch the shadows change
I cannot help but think
Of how much beauty we fail to see
In the shifting shades of natural things

Sometimes I wonder
if the answers
have always been there

Waiting

And all along
I have simply been getting
the questions wrong

Within the realm of things I love
Are knotted pines and mourning doves
Life in bloom on crooked paths
The shifting stones of riverbeds
Feral ways of winter days
And knowing the winds will always change

I have been more owl
than dove
More shadowed pine
than olive branch
And sharpness holds
its place in the world
but for now
I would like to soften
the bark of my flesh
and allow the taste
of sweeter words
to find their place
upon my breath

Nothing in nature lasts forever
The weather
The seasons
The rise and fall of daylight
There is a cadence to it all
A rhythm in tune
with things beyond our reach

And yet

There is chaos among the chorus
An unpredictability
as to how many different ways
the drum beats of life
may ebb and change
As to how many precious moments
will end up taking
your breath away

The season of heartache
is slow to fade
But just as the leaves
shall grow again
on branches stripped bare
when the cold settled in
Buds of hope
shall take their place
in the hearts of those
Who had lost their way

I used to believe that suffering
in the aftermath of someone else's actions
was a result of all their faults
I used to believe that they owed me
an explanation
as a step towards closure
or at the very least, a basic apology

But I have learned
these past few years
that people behave in ways
that reflect their own demons
Actions are a mirror to the heart
and I will gain nothing
from focusing on someone else's reflection

My soul is independent of theirs
and the only closure I need pursue
Is the mending of my own internal wounds
Suffering is an experience
that paves the way for greater growth

It is mine to keep
It is mine to own

I have no interest
in changing the past
Pain breeds creativity
and I am a lover
of things that cannot last
So words shall flow
from within my veins
as long as ashes
are born of flames

A starving heart
can survive on slivers of touch
Crumbs of affection licked from the floor
Years of begging for morsels more

In time the soul becomes a sponge
Soaking in drops of halfway love
Settling into indifferent acceptance
as shrinking needs collect layers of dust

But what a way to inch through life
On hands and needs for essential things
when we were designed
for full belly nights

So let us refuse to merely sustain
but declare our hunger with open eyes
Run towards the ones with abundance to give
With wine on their lips and feasts in their arms

Today I wrote a eulogy
to the version of me
who was lost at sea
To the woman left rigid
by a winter of sorrow
who sank into an abysmal sleep
and gave up hope
on the dawn of tomorrows
I praised her
for the years she spent
surviving on gulps
of thinning breaths
For the fire she summoned
when the world was black
For the layers she lost
as they clawed at her back
That version of me
is dead and gone
Replaced with the face
of a woman reborn

A woman who knows
she is worth so much more

The fates have no faith in forever
Only in each moment in time
Finding its place as the stars align

Jennifer Gordon

I have loved you more
than you will ever know
So much so
that the scent of you
will ever linger
in the soil of my soul

There is so much pain
in loss
In losing the ones
we love
But in the eye of
the storm
I am at peace
knowing
that the things
I need
are all still here
inside of me

Sometimes
survival depends
on letting go
When your only hope
of reaching the shore
is to open your fists
and begin to swim

I bathe in waves of darkness
Lay in caves of hollowed hearts
Soak the sadness of the world
In through open pores
And from the shadows on my face
I knit a quilt of softer days
Take the pain of moments lost
Of heavy souls and graveyard bones
Place their weight upon my chest
To lend the ebb of lulling breaths
For I am a magician in female form
The one who dares to calm the storm

It is in the nature
of deeper thinkers
To view the ledge
with curiosity
To inch their toes
beyond the edge
Simply to study
the rush of things
that rise
To embrace the occasion
of temptation
Knowing the meaning
of a beautiful life
is to truly feel alive

I am the moth who is drawn by light
Are we not all so simple and small?
But others reach for sunlit days
While I am a lover of burning flames

After all this time
light as begun
to peak in through the cracks
and I can tell my soul
is unsure
of how it should react

There has only been darkness
Only sadness for years
and it burns to open my eyes
To take in the view
of an unfamiliar sky

Inevitably
at daybreak you shall
find me
Savoring the warmth
of sleep
And lamenting the loss
of dreams
worth saving

I have not loved you any less
since the day you walked away
All I can think
is how beautiful you are
even from a distance

Grief has settled
upon my skin
So I leave the scent
of sadness in my wake
And I hope one day
our paths will cross
and the fragrance takes
your breath away

I had always believed
that every emotion
had an expiration
But your presence
in this world
has shown me
that connection
in its purest form
is a remarkable exception

Always
I will be my own home
Speaking kindly to my soul
And I will vow
To embrace my warmth
Wrap myself in open arms
For over time
I have come to see
I deserved to be loved
By the hands that hold me

Jennifer Gordon

Learn to love yourself first
Get to know the contents of your soul
Because in the end there is nothing worse
That letting time run out
While you are still a stranger to yourself

The magic of growth
is found in watching
what was once a stone
inside your hand
take the form of a feather
upon your back

What a tragedy
How we underestimate
the resilience of the human soul

Undermining survival mode
Strength and grit awaiting awakening
lurking just below rock bottom

We allow the crushing of our will
let them grind our tenacity to bits
to broken molds, scattered stones

All because we are wrongly told
that our nature is to crumble
and mortal bones are weak in structure

Lacking whatever it is
that gods and drugs may offer

And like the marigolds
Pruned for growth
I will bloom brighter
After every cut

Somehow my soul
has found new roots
And I'm not quite sure
how these petals grew
But I do know
There was no you
before the bloom

Sometimes joy
is a slow growing vine
Taking more time
than our hearts would like
to wind its way over walls of pain
Inching along
towards lighter days

Jennifer Gordon

I lie awake in cotton sheets
Longing to rest my limbs
On a forest floor of fallen leaves

My soul is stained by wisdom's ink
Drips of brilliance
from rivers trickled upon my cheeks
And I can laugh with ghosts of the past
as we dance together
on the ashes of moments
that were never meant to last

In the desperation of darkest moments
We learn to ignite our inner light
And from the bottom of the pit
Our brokenness finds the strength to climb

Most days
Healing feels like
Finding balance
Between the hours
Of suppression
And little moments
Of self-expression

When you put in the work
To believe in yourself
The opinions of others
Will begin to lose
Their illusion of worth

My hope is that we
can embrace ourselves

Come home to the hearts
which warm our chests

Love the mess
The imperfect flesh

Know our worth
and release the rest

Jennifer Gordon

I have never feared
surviving the storm
It is the years
that slowly pass
without feeling
the rain upon my back
that threaten to
break my soul

Search for me
in shallow waters
And you will find
remnants
I have left behind
Shedded
Floating and forgotten
Abandoned by
a woman inclined
to swim out towards
the open sea

Slowly
I am searching the earth
for pieces of me
swept away
by the winds of grief

I am in no hurry

I know
that healing is a journey
and I plan to savor
the adventure of
rebuilding

And if the beatings of my heart
Should find themselves again one day
Struggling for the strength to carry on
I will wait on no one's empathy
I will hold myself in loving arms
Remembering
How darkness always leads to dawn

Epilogue

I cringe a little inside, every time I hear someone dismissively give the advice to "let it go". Because most often, there is no "it." There may have been a loss…or an incident…or a betrayal, but the aftermath of those moments is so much more than singular. Telling someone to let it go implies that they have closed their fist around a solitary emotion and that they have the ability to set it down. As if the experience of pain or loss hasn't changed who they are. As if they have the choice to detach themselves from something that has become a part of the lens through which they see the world. So instead of expecting people to release whatever "it" is that weighs them down, start by loving people wherever they are. Acknowledge that their experience is separate from yours and has affected them in ways you do not understand. The only way to truly heal, is not to force a separation, but to accept and absorb the things that have changed them. From the point of acceptance, one can begin to grow, to determine the shapes these things will take. So be the one who offers love and kindness. Be the one who allows someone the space they need, to do the work within themselves that will heal them from the inside out.

This book is dedicated to the distance
that stretches from the ocean floor
to the stars adorning heaven's door.

www.ingramcontent.com/pod-product-compliance
Lightning Source LLC
Chambersburg PA
CBHW070724130626
46553CB00005B/2141